Stonehenge

BY ELIZABETH RAUM

Amicus High Interest is an imprint of Amicus
P.O. Box 1329, Mankato, MN 56002
www.amicuspublishing.us

Library of Congress Cataloging-in-Publication Data
Raum, Elizabeth.
 Stonehenge / by Elizabeth Raum.
     pages cm. – (Ancient wonders)
 Includes bibliographical references and index.
 Summary: "Describes the mysteries behind Stonehenge,
including how and why it was built, the people who built it, and
what the ruins are like today"–Provided by publisher.
 ISBN 978-1-60753-469-3 (library binding) –
 ISBN 978-1-60753-684-0 (ebook)
 1. Stonehenge (England)–Juvenile literature. 2. Wiltshire
(England)–Antiquities–Juvenile literature. 3. Megalithic
monuments–England–Wiltshire–Juvenile literature. I. Title.
 DA142.R38 2015
 936.2'319–dc23
                                                  2013028298

Editors   Kristina Ericksen and Rebecca Glaser
Series Designer   Kathleen Petelinsek
Book Designer   Heather Dreisbach
Photo Researcher   Kurtis Kinneman

Photo Credits
Shutterstock/Borna_Mirahmadian, cover; Shutterstock/Pecold,
5; Superstock/Robert Harding Picture Library, 6; Alamy/Arcaid
Images, 9; Alamy/Keith Morris, 10; Shutterstock/Stephen
Inglis, 13; Getty Images/ Tetra Images, 14; Superstock, 17;
Alamy/National Geographic Image Collection, 18; Alamy/
Chronicle, 21; Superstock/David Nunuk/All Canada Photos,
23; Superstock/Nomad, 25; Alamy/ Katharine Andriotis, 26;
Superstock/Robert Harding Picture Library, 29

Printed in the United States of America at Corporate Graphics
in North Mankato, Minnesota.

10 9 8 7 6 5 4 3 2 1

Table of Contents

Stone Mystery

Stonehenge is the world's most famous stone circle. It has been standing in England for thousands of years. Stonehenge is a mystery. **Archaeologists** study and dig around the stones. They explore the mysteries of this ancient wonder. Why was it built? What did people do there?

The stones at Stonehenge are much taller than a person.

Stonehenge is in southern England on Salisbury Plain. It is near the city of Salisbury. It is a two-hour drive from London. The land is flat. There are few trees. Rivers and streams run through it. Early British people settled here. They farmed the land. They herded sheep. About 5,000 years ago, they began building Stonehenge.

From above, you can see an inner and an outer circle.

These ancient people believed circles had special powers. They built **henges** at important sites. A henge is a circle of raised earth. It also has a ditch. Archaeologists have found about 350 henges and buildings on Salisbury Plain. Stonehenge is the most famous.

 How did ancient people dig the henges?

This henge in northern England is about 295 ft (90 m) across.

 They used picks made of animal bones as shovels.

The bluestones used for Stonehenge came from this area near Wales.

 Are bluestones blue?

Building Stonehenge

Stonehenge was built over hundreds of years. First, workers dug the circular wall, or henge. It has a ditch with high banks inside. It has low banks outside.

Next, they dug 56 pits inside the henge. They probably put bluestones in them. These stone slabs came from Wales. No one knows how they got to England.

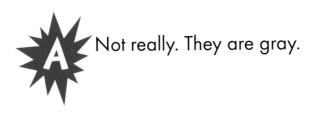 Not really. They are gray.

After the henge was built, work stopped. About 300 years later, people started changing Stonehenge. They brought in big sandstone blocks called **sarsen**. They smoothed them with hammers. The stones are 13 to 23 feet (4 to 7 m) high. They weigh up to 40 tons, or 80,000 pounds (36,287 kg) each. That's as much as eight female elephants.

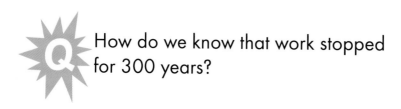

How do we know that work stopped for 300 years?

Large sandstone blocks were added years after Stonehenge was built.

 Archaeologists use **carbon dating** to find out how old something is. They can tell that parts of Stonehenge have different ages.

We do not know how workers moved the heavy stones into trilithons.

 Q What happened to the missing stones?

Workers placed two sarsen blocks next to one another. They put a third on top. This made a **trilithon**. They put five in a horseshoe shape. They put bluestones around it. Then they added an outer circle of trilithons. Some of the stones have fallen. Some are now missing.

 Weather damaged some. Others may have been stolen. We don't know for sure.

Looking for Clues

Workers made changes for the next 500 years. They stopped around 1600 BC. That's almost 3,500 years ago! People worked on Stonehenge for 1,500 years. Over time, they deserted it. No one knows why. All communities change over time. The people living near Stonehenge changed, too.

An artist painted Stonehenge
as it looked in the 1800s.

This drawing shows how ancient people in England might have lived.

 Why is Durrington Walls important?

In 2007, archaeologists made a discovery. They uncovered another ruin near Stonehenge. It is called Durrington Walls. It was an ancient village. It sits inside a henge. Archaeologists think hundreds of workers lived there. The wooden walls of their houses have rotted away. But the floors remain.

 It may give clues about the people who built Stonehenge.

The Purpose

Stonehenge workers did not read or write. They left no written records. In the 1600s, John Aubrey began the first study of Stonehenge. He mapped the ruin. He discovered five strange holes. We call them Aubrey Holes. Later, scientists uncovered 51 more Aubrey Holes.

John Aubrey was the first to study and write about Stonehenge.

People probably gathered at
Stonehenge at special times.

Archaeologists dug into the holes. They found burned human bones. Stonehenge was once used as a cemetery. People honored their **ancestors** there. They probably met during the **summer solstice** and **winter solstice**. That's when seasons change. Stonehenge has been used many ways through the years.

Some archaeologists think that Stonehenge may have been a giant stone calendar. Certain stones line up with the sun on the summer and winter solstices. People may have used the stones to predict **solar eclipses**. Others think Stonehenge might have been an ancient hospital. People may have believed that the bluestones had magical healing powers.

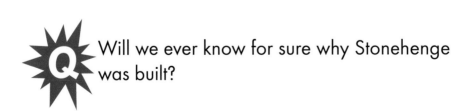
Q Will we ever know for sure why Stonehenge was built?

A solar eclipse happens when the moon blocks our view of the sun.

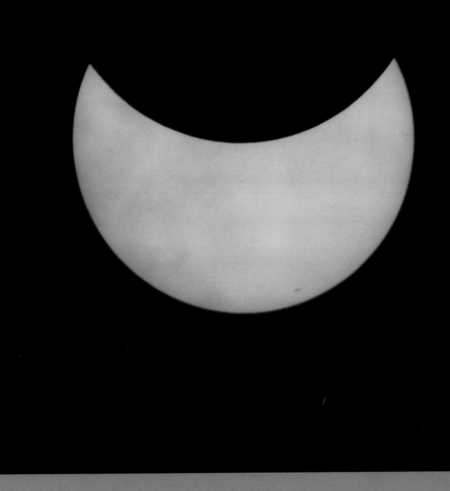

 Probably not. But archaeologists will keep digging for new clues.

Tourists travel to England to see the circle of stones.

Visiting Stonehenge

More than a million people visit Stonehenge each year. They come from all over. During most tours, visitors cannot touch the giant stones. Ropes keep people back. Then the stones won't get damaged. Special access tours let people go inside the stone circle. Tourists must buy tickets months ahead of time to get inside.

Thousands visit Stonehenge for the summer solstice. It's the beginning of summer. At noon on June 20 or 21, the sun is directly overhead. It's the longest day of the year. People visit Stonehenge to celebrate.

The ropes are down. Anyone can touch the stones. Stonehenge seems magical. It's a celebration of ancient wonders!

People come to Stonehenge to celebrate the summer solstice.

Glossary

ancestor A relative who lived many years ago.

archaeologist A scientist who studies the remains of ancient people.

carbon dating A method of testing wood, leather, and bones to find out how old something is.

henge A circular bank of raised earth that includes a ditch.

sarsen A sandstone block used for building.

solar eclipse When the moon comes between the sun and the earth.

summer solstice The day when the sun is closest to the earth, usually about June 21; the longest day of the year.

trilithon A structure made from three stones, with two upright and the third on top.

winter solstice The day when the sun is farthest from the earth, usually about December 21; the shortest day of the year.

Read More

Aronson, Marc. *If Stones Could Speak: Unlocking the Secrets of Stonehenge.* Washington, D.C.: National Geographic, 2010.

Hawkins, John. *The World's Strangest Unexplained Mysteries.* New York: PowerKids Press, 2012.

Henzel, Cynthia Kennedy. *Stonehenge.* Edina, Minn.: ABDO Pub. Co., 2011.

Websites

About Stonehenge
http://www.stonehenge.co.uk/about.php

BBC News | Science/Nature | Building of Stonehenge
http://news.bbc.co.uk/2/hi/science/nature/7322444.stm

Kids Discover Stonehenge
http://www.kidsdiscover.com/blog/spotlight/stonehenge-for-kids/

Every effort has been made to ensure that these websites are appropriate for children. However, because of the nature of the Internet, it is impossible to guarantee that these sites will remain active indefinitely or that their contents will not be altered.

Index

About the Author

Elizabeth Raum has worked as a teacher, librarian, and writer. She has written dozens of books for young readers. She likes doing research and learning about new topics. After writing about ancient wonders, she wants to travel the world to visit them! To learn more, visit her website at www.elizabethraum.net.